STAYING GROUNDED
Restoring the Ancient Practices

PARTICIPANT'S GUIDE

Q Group Studies

Five Sessions

GABE LYONS AND NORTON HERBST

 ZONDERVAN®

ZONDERVAN.com/
AUTHORTRACKER
follow your favorite authors

ZONDERVAN

Q Study: Staying Grounded Participant's Guide
Copyright © 2011 by Q

Requests for information should be addressed to:
Zondervan, *Grand Rapids, Michigan 49530*

ISBN 978-0-310-67136-7

Published in association with Yates & Yates, www.yates2.com.

Printed in the United States of America

11 12 13 14 15 16 /DCI/ 32 31 30 29 28 27 26 25 24 23 22 21 20 19 18 17 16 15 14 13 12 11 10 9 8 7 6 5 4 3 2 1

TABLE OF CONTENTS

—

STAYING GROUNDED: RESTORING THE ANCIENT PRACTICES

It's no secret that we live in a fast-paced world. It seems that everything is always changing: from the political climate and the economy to where we live, what we do, and how quickly our kids grow up. Add to this how fast technology changes and it seems like we're constantly forced to buy new gadgets, learn new tools, and upgrade our software just to keep up. If we don't become more efficient, produce more dollars, get ahead, and stay ahead, then we'll certainly be left behind.

For people on a mission to make an impact in culture, the tendencies can be even stronger. We strive so hard to make a difference, but in the midst of all our tireless work and busyness, it's easy to drift away from the foundation of our faith. Without even noticing it, we become disconnected from God and our overarching role in the world. And when all the things in our lives start to lose their fulfillment—our jobs, relationships, purchases, and busy schedules—we wonder where we got off track and lost our bearings.

In this Q Study, your group will explore how recovering the ancient practices of our faith can be our anchor in an often-chaotic world. You'll consider several habits in particular that Christians have practiced throughout the centuries. You'll also discuss how these habits require patient discipline—something our culture rebels against. But ultimately, you'll discover that they aren't optional; the practices *are* the foundation by which we ground our faith.

STAYING GROUNDED
WELCOME

WELCOME TO Q STUDIES

Q Studies are designed to convene small groups of people to dialogue, learn, and work together to help you navigate the tensions of following Jesus in a post-Christian culture. Q Studies are actually based on an old idea—the Society Rooms of the late 1600s. These small gatherings of leaders that would convene, dialogue, learn, and work together to strengthen their faith and renew their culture. Consider the impact of these early Society Rooms:

> In 1673 Dr. Anthony Horneck, a Church of England minister in London, preached a number of what he called "awakening sermons." As a result several young men began to meet together weekly in order to build up one another in the Christian faith. They gathered in small groups at certain fixed locations and their places of meeting became known as Society Rooms. In these gatherings they read the Bible, studied religious books and prayed; they also went out among the poor to relieve want at their own expense and to show kindness to all. By 1730 nearly one hundred of these Societies existed in London, and others—perhaps another hundred—were to be found in cities and towns throughout England. The Societies movement became, in many senses, the cradle of the Revival … (Arnold Dallimore, *George Whitefield*, Vol 1., Crossway, 1990, pp. 28–29)

Following this historical example, this Q Study is designed to renew your minds as leaders so that you can live out your faith and make a difference in society. As you begin meeting together, your group should be characterized by a commitment to put learning into action. And no doubt, over the course of the next few weeks, your innermost beliefs and preconceived ideas about life, faith, the world, and your cultural responsibility will be challenged. But that's the point.

Here's how it works. Your group will gather five times to discuss important topics related to the overall theme of this study. Sometimes you'll be given something to do or read before your group gathers. It's important for you to take these "assignments" seriously. They won't demand much time, but they will require intentionality. Doing these things ahead of time will cultivate a richer and more stimulating group experience as you begin to practice what you are learning.

For each group gathering, set aside about one hour and fifteen minutes for the discussion in a place with minimal distractions. Your group may want to share a meal together first, but be sure to allow enough time for unhurried dialogue to take place. Sometimes you'll watch a short video. But conversation and dialogue will always be the priority. The leader of the group will not teach or lecture, but instead will ask questions, facilitate conversation, and seek input from everyone. Be prepared to ask good questions and share your own thoughts. Sometimes you'll even debate an issue by taking sides and thinking through all the complexities. The goal of each gathering is for your group to be stimulated by a particular idea and learn together as you discuss its impact on your faith, your lives, and culture in general. Your group may not arrive at a consensus regarding any given topic. That's okay. Be respectful of others, even when you disagree with them. We can learn something from everyone.

Before your fifth gathering, you will undertake a group project together. You may be tempted to skip this. Don't! Your group project might be the most important part of your experience. Genuine learning as a community takes place when you *engage* the ideas you are discussing and *do* something together as a group.

In the end, be committed to this group and the learning process that is about to ensue. Your willingness to prepare for group gatherings, keep an open mind, and demonstrate eagerness to learn together will pave the way for a great experience.

YOUR PLACE IN CULTURE

INTRODUCTIONS

At the beginning of your first gathering, spend about fifteen minutes introducing yourselves to one another and discussing your channel of cultural influence.

There are several different social institutions that touch every person in a given society. These areas of influence contain most of the industries and organizations that consistently shape our culture. They touch every aspect of our lives, and most of us find our vocational roles in one or more of these areas. They are the seven channels of cultural influence.

As you begin your Q Study experience, you'll notice that most, if not all, of these channels are represented in your group. Start your first gathering by sharing which particular channel of influence you participate in. Give the rest of the group a sense of how your channel contributes to shaping society in general. Then, throughout the rest of the group experience, reflect on how your learning will affect the channel to which you've been called.

7

Channels of Cultural Influence

01

m

media

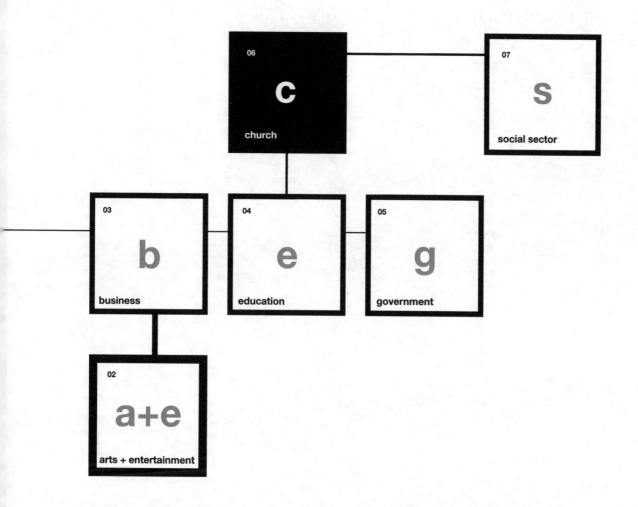

Man must be disciplined, for he is by nature
raw and wild.

IMMANUEL KANT

We learn by practice. Whether it means
to learn to dance by practicing dancing
or to learn to live by practicing living, the
principles are the same. One becomes in
some area an athlete of God.

MARTHA GRAHAM

This is what the Lord says:
"Stand at the crossroads and look;
        ask for the ancient paths,
ask where the good way is, and walk in it,
        and you will find rest for your souls."

JEREMIAH 6:16

RECOVERING THE ANCIENT PRACTICES

THE HABITS OF YOUR FAITH

DISCUSS

Spend a few minutes sharing your thoughts with the group.

Habits reveal what we believe, who we are, and what's most important to us. Take your finances, for example. How do you spend your money? Are you carrying significant debt? Do you balance your checkbook? Do you regularly save or give? How you answer these questions reveals your financial habits. And your financial habits reveal your financial priorities.

It's no different with faith. So, what are the habits by which you express and nurture your faith?

DISCUSSION STARTERS

Is attending church an important habit for you?

What do you do during the week to stay grounded in your faith?

Are you a disciplined person that likes order and consistency, or are you someone who "flies by the seat of your pants"?

What do you think are the three most important things you can do regularly to express or nurture your faith?

HABITS OF AMERICAN CHRISTIANS

Frequency of Attendance at Religious Services Among American Christians

U.S. Religious Traditions	More than once a week	Once a week	Once or twice a month	A few times a year	Seldom	Never	Don't know/ refused
Evangelical churches	30%	28%	14%	14%	9%	4%	1%
Mainline churches	8%	26%	19%	23%	16%	7%	1%
Historically black churches	30%	29%	16%	13%	9%	3%	1%
Catholics	9%	33%	19%	20%	13%	6%	0%
Orthodox	8%	26%	21%	28%	12%	4%	1%
Other Christians	8%	19%	21%	19%	14%	17%	1%

Frequency of Prayer Among American Christians

U.S. Religious Traditions	Daily	Weekly	Monthly	Seldom	Never	Don't know/ refused
Evangelical churches	78%	14%	3%	4%	1%	1%
Mainline churches	53%	23%	7%	12%	3%	2%
Historically black churches	80%	12%	2%	3%	1%	2%
Catholics	58%	21%	7%	10%	3%	1%
Orthodox	60%	17%	5%	12%	4%	2%
Other Christians	71%	16%	2%	7%	3%	2%

Source: The Pew Forum on Religion & Public Life: "U.S. Religious Landscape Survey: Diverse and Politically Relevant," June 2008 at http://religions.pewforum.org/reports#.

RECOVERING THE ANCIENT PRACTICES

View Q Talk: Recovering the Ancient Practices by Phyllis Tickle.

Record your thoughts on the talk on page 15.

Phyllis Tickle is founding editor of the Religion Department of *Publishers Weekly*, the international journal of the book industry, and is an authority on religion in America. In addition to lectures and numerous essays, articles, and interviews, Tickle is the author of over two dozen books on religion and spirituality, most recently *The Great Emergence* and *How Christianity Is Changing*. She is also the general editor of the Ancient Practices Series.

In the busyness of life today, many Christians lose sight of the disciplines, or practices, that keep them grounded. Participating in culture as salt and light demands an anchor point found only in the disciplined life. At Q Chicago, Phyllis Tickle shared how seven historic practices in particular carry serious countercultural weight in a consumer-driven society.

—

"Our first obligation is to be citizens of the kingdom of God. And that is to say we are called upon to do those things that so completely shape our life that our citizenship is absolutely obvious."

—

"So [we practice] the liturgical year, reminding ourselves, reminding our children, reminding our community that this is the story we live every day of our lives and we measure our time by it."

—

"You can't intellectualize faith. Faith is the thing you do incarnate."

—

"One of the things that contemporary Christianity lacks is transcendence."

THOUGHTS

DISCIPLINES AND CHECKLISTS

DEBATE

Split the group into two sides and spend fifteen minutes debating the issue:

Is there a danger in adopting regular practices out of a sense of duty and determination rather than letting our connection with God develop naturally, organically, and when we are genuinely motivated to pursue him?

Even if you don't agree with the side you are representing, consider and offer the best arguments for your position. Be respectful.

Record your thoughts on pages 18-19.

Use the following debate starters to guide your time.

In the past, Christians incorporated the kinds of disciplines that Phyllis Tickle described into the rhythms of their lives in order to nurture their faith. But for some, these types of practices encouraged a checklist mentality: "do these things to be a good Christian." Consequently, many contemporary Christians have sworn off anything that smells of a ritualistic checklist and instead pursued a faith that is "organic," "Spirit-led in the moment," and, in their opinions, not "works-based."

Is there a danger in adopting regular practices out of a sense of duty and determination rather than letting our connection with God develop naturally, organically, and when we are genuinely motivated to pursue him?

DEBATE STARTERS

Should we adopt disciplines that we don't particularly enjoy practicing at first?

When do disciplines become unhealthy obligations?

Regarding the discipline of financial giving, Paul instructs Christians to "give what you have decided in your heart to give, not reluctantly or under compulsion, for God loves a cheerful giver" (2 Cor. 9:7). Does this suggest that disciplines should never be practiced under obligation? Why or why not?

If genuine motivation is lacking, how does one even begin to nurture one's faith on a regular basis?

—

YES

Our connection with God should develop naturally, organically, and when we are genuinely motivated to pursue him.

THOUGHTS

—

NO

Practices require some elements of duty, determination, and discipline because genuine motivation is often lacking.

THOUGHTS

THE SEVEN ANCIENT PRACTICES

Have a few people in your group take turns reading this section aloud.

In her presentation, Phyllis Tickle described seven ancient practices that faithful followers have incorporated into their lives for thousands of years. Their origins are found in the narratives of Hebrew people in the Old Testament and the teachings of Jesus' followers in the New Testament. And in every generation since, Christians have found purpose, meaning, and fulfillment in their use.

Three of the practices relate to our physical bodies:

1. *Tithing* is the habit of giving away a percentage of one's income—that which is normally used to provide for one's physical needs.
2. *Communion*, or the *Lord's Supper*, or *Eucharist*, or *Mass*, is the physical meal that we regularly share together to celebrate Christ's atoning death on the cross.
3. *Fasting* is the regular giving up of food that one needs to sustain health.

The other four practices govern or measure our relationship to time:

4. *Fixed-hour prayer* incorporates daily time spent with God into the life of the believer.

5. *Observing the Sabbath* regulates the rest we need on a weekly basis.

6. *Following the liturgical calendar*, both in public worship and private devotion, provides rhythm to our year as we relive the story of God's redemptive act in history through Jesus.

7. *Pilgrimage* marks a few journeys during one's life to a sacred or hallowed place.

REFLECTION STARTERS

Spend a few minutes journaling your thoughts to the two questions below. Then, share your reflections with the group.

Of these practices, which is the most unfamiliar or odd to you? Why?

Which of these practices—one that you currently do not observe regularly— would be possible for you to begin this week? What would it take to begin?

JOURNAL

JOURNAL

OUR OWN LOVE FOR GOD

ACT

Faith is not simply intellectual belief in Jesus' atoning work. It certainly includes that, but more importantly, it's something we *practice*. By incorporating regular habits into our lives, we train our bodies, minds, and wills in such a way that, in Paul's words, we become "conformed to the image of [Christ]" (Rom. 8:29). Sometimes these habits will come naturally with a genuine desire to grow in our intimacy with God. Oftentimes, they won't. But the goal is not a checklist of obligatory rules by which we earn God's love. The ultimate goal is a reciprocal expression of our own love for God and his redemptive mission for our world.

Which particular ancient practice will you begin incorporating into your life this week?

—

FROM PURCHASES TO PRACTICES

—

Before your next gathering, read the Q Short by Andy Crouch beginning on page 28. Be sure to set aside some uninterrupted time for this. Try not to save it until the last minute. When you read the essay, underline, highlight, or jot down comments about ideas (on page 43) that are particularly interesting, disconcerting, or challenging. Be prepared to share why at the next gathering.

FROM PURCHASES TO PRACTICES

FROM PURCHASES TO PRACTICES
By Andy Crouch

A few years ago someone observed to me that when you read American newspapers from the turn of the last century, you commonly see a word that now seems a bit quaint. When journalists from the late 1800s wanted to refer collectively to the 76 million Americans alive at that time, they called them *citizens*.

But by the turn of the millennium, a different word had become our customary way of speaking of Americans as a whole—300 million of us today. Now, more often than not, the word that appears to designate us is *consumers*.

Practically speaking, the word *consumer* didn't exist in 1900. For one thing, there wasn't very much to consume. Richard Sears had just launched his catalog in 1894. What people consumed, they tended to produce—40 percent of the population were farmers, compared to 2 percent today. Meanwhile, the word *citizen* had tremendous resonance in a coun-

try that had just concluded its first century of existence, under a new form of government that relied in unprecedented ways on the participation of ordinary people. Our nation had suffered a wrenching civil war that required Americans to decide what kind of nation they would inhabit, and what kind of citizens they would be. No wonder that when our great- or great-great-grandparents thought of themselves, they thought of themselves as citizens.

When we further recall that in 1900 women had not yet been given the right to vote, we realize that the actual number of fully enfranchised "citizens" was probably well below 30 million. That's still a large number, but it's much easier to envision yourself as a citizen who can actually make a difference in a country of 30 million than in a country of 300 million. And most Americans at the time lived not in cities but in rural areas or small towns, close to the mechanics of local government. These days, when we do talk about civic participation, we use the word *voters*. But *voter*, compared to *citizen*, probably would have seemed to our great-greatgrandparents a very thin word indeed.

Those great-great-grandparents could not possibly have anticipated the century's worth of economic growth in the 1900s that would introduce a profusion of consumer goods to the average citizen of the developed world. This year, 300,000 books will be published in the United States. More than 100,000 films are currently available from Netflix—if you watched one every night, it would take 273 years to get through the whole catalog. One of the greatest psychological challenges the typical middle-class resident of America now faces, as documented by psychologists like Barry Schwartz, is simply the abundance of choice. We have become adept at minutely examining and excavating our own preferences and needs, from what toothpaste to use to what movie to rank in our Netflix queue, and leveraging the worldwide power of brands to carve out our own sense of identity. In a typical week, even in a presidential election year, how many times do you communicate with one of your elected representatives or participate in a public meeting? And how many times do you

order that particular combination of customized drink at your local coffeeshop that defines you as *you*? It's no wonder that we call ourselves consumers.

This dramatic shift in the way we name ourselves does not mean, obviously, that we have stopped being citizens. It just means that on a daily basis, the place where we find meaning and satisfaction is not primarily in civic participation, but in consumption. Citizenship seems remote and impersonal; consumption seems immediate and individual, something we can actively do to shape our world. Perhaps it's not surprising that when Al Qaeda unleashed its horrific challenge to America, the clarion call from the White House was, "Go shopping." We are still citizens, but many of us find our identity, who we are, even our response to the most pressing issues of our time, in what we consume.

SATISFACTION

There are many differences between a culture built around consumption and a culture built around citizenship, but the one that fascinates me most is consumer culture's ability to give us nearly instantaneous experiences of satisfaction. A few weeks ago I read a blog post about a new musical artist who blends classical piano, trip-hop, and ambient music. Within minutes I had found him on iTunes, downloaded his album, and pressed play. The gap between desire and satisfaction was almost imperceptible, allowing for just a bit of pleasurable anticipation as the spinning cursor indicated the swift progress of my download.

Indeed, as any serious shopper can tell you, the satisfaction began even before I clicked on the "buy this album" button in iTunes. Anticipation itself was quite satisfying. My satisfaction notched up further when I put in my earphones, pressed play, and started to immerse myself in an elaborate new musical world. Given how painlessly I was parted from my money (Apple kindly stores my credit card details on their server—aren't they nice?), it was, so far, a perfectly satisfying experience. You could draw it on a simple graph—satisfaction over time—like this:

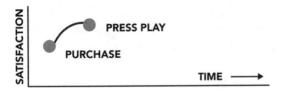

But I knew even before I pressed play that this album, no matter how good it turned out to be, was very unlikely to stay as satisfying as it was on that first hearing. True, the second or fourth or tenth time I listened to it I might still be hearing new details in the music or appreciating some subtle resonance in the lyrics. But eventually, if this album followed the pattern of nearly every one of the thousands of pieces of recorded music I have bought in my lifetime, the satisfaction would start to trail off:

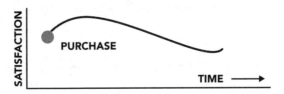

We've all had this experience. Before you bought it, the album seemed like something you couldn't live without. And at first it delivers thrilling new experiences. But as it becomes more and more part of your routine, eventually it subsides into the background, gathering digital dust in the depths of your iTunes list, delivering very little additional satisfaction. Go back far enough in your history of musical purchases, at least when you reach a certain age, and some of them start to seem downright *unsatisfying*: great was my embarrassment when a friend paging through my iTunes collection found Journey's *Greatest Hits*, with a surprisingly high play count for "Faithfully." (Tenth grade, slow dance, Julie Tucker—you had to be there.)

This is, in fact, the normal pattern for consumer goods: they deliver most of the satisfaction right up front. The moment you drive the car off the lot; the opening chase scene of the latest James Bond movie; the first bite of the Wendy's Baconator—all are carefully designed to drive your satisfaction-ometer right off the chart. *Sustaining* satisfaction, though, is not a high priority for the producers of consumer goods, for a simple reason. There is just one economic transaction that takes place: the initial purchase. After that transaction is over, it's actually in the best interests of the producer that your satisfaction trail off, because the way consumers deal with declining satisfaction is to make another purchase:

In essence, life in a consumer society works this way: frequent experiences of up-front satisfaction, followed by fairly rapid fall-offs in satisfaction, which are compensated for by fresh purchases. Lather, rinse, repeat.

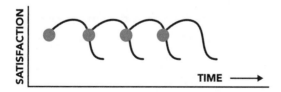

Now, as long as you have the money to keep making those purchases, this pattern works. You stay satisfied at a very high level, constantly enthralled by the newest and greatest. And you keep a bunch of companies in business. And indeed, there is something elemental about this pattern: it is, after all, the pattern of one of the most basic human experiences, hunger. We eat, are satisfied, grow hungry, and eat again. The genius of consumer culture is to extend this basic human experience to almost every corner of our lives: the cars we drive, the television we watch, the websites we visit. Call it the *pattern of purchases*. In a consumer economy, this is the template for more and more of our discretionary money and time: satisfaction sustained by frequent purchases. All it really requires of us is money.

But truth be told, rarely does a pattern of purchases deliver a consistently high level of satisfaction. Consider this:

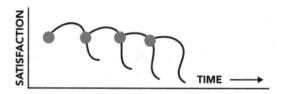

In this pattern, which is obviously a close cousin of the previous one, there is the same frequently repeated series of purchases, but instead of satisfaction remaining at a consistently high level, it dips with each subsequent purchase, never getting back to the original level of satisfaction.

This, of course, is the pattern of addiction.

The addict, like the consumer, purchases some good that initially delivers tremendous satisfaction—in the case of the most impressive psychoactive drugs, a feeling of euphoria that is consistently described as the most extraordinary moment in the users' lives. The effect, however, wears off relatively quickly. Eager to recapture that experience, the user makes another purchase. This time around, though, the effect is subtly not quite as powerful, and perhaps it wears off more quickly—prompting another purchase, which while still satisfying, is just a bit less so. And on it goes. Lather, rinse, repeat. But the worst addictions don't just level off at a depressing (and expensive) steady state of minimal satisfaction. To depict them we have to extend our y-axis into negative territory:

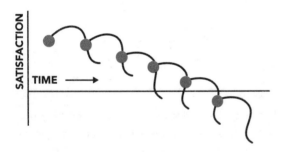

In the long run, with the most addictive substances and behaviors, the satisfaction from each additional unit is actually negative—*un*-satisfying and destructive—yet the user is so entrenched in the pattern, still clinging to the memory of those first euphoric hits, that he or she is unable to escape. With the worst addictions, apart from the grace of God, the pattern always and only ends in the premature death of the user, caught in a downward spiral that began with beautiful bliss.

PRACTICES

There is, however, another path toward satisfaction that is different altogether from the reward curve of purchases and addictions, and some of us were fortunate to discover it early on. We can illustrate it with a very different kind of play: not playing a CD or an MP3, but playing a musical instrument—say, a violin.

What happens when we begin to play the violin, the first time we pick up that beautifully crafted instrument and draw the bow across the strings? Well, I have an eight-year-old daughter studying violin right now, and I can tell you that first moment of play definitely does not produce satisfaction. The instrument screeches. It's horribly out of tune. Cats all over the neighborhood run for cover. When you start to play the violin, you start out deep in negative satisfaction.

And that's where you stay for quite awhile.

Day after day, month after month, every time you try to play the violin, it is work—hard, slow, unsatisfying work. For the first year or more, the satisfaction curve pretty much looks like this:

But, if you keep at it, practicing daily, enduring the screeches and squawks, the out-of-tune notes, the tired left hand and the sore right arm, eventually, one day, maybe a few years down the road, you pick up the violin and something satisfying happens.

You're not Itzhak Perlman, not by a long shot, but you play something that sounds like, well, music—rich and lovely and alive.

And if you keep practicing, your satisfaction starts to gradually lift off from the very slight satisfactions of keeping notes in tune and occasionally coaxing a decent tone out of the instrument, to the satisfactions of being able to play whole pieces with something that approaches grace.

And here's the really interesting thing about the satisfaction curve associated with learning to play the violin, so very different from playing an MP3. It keeps going up for a very long time. It may never go down. My wife Catherine played violin as a child, then set it aside as school and work and family took up her time. But when our daughter started studying violin, Catherine picked her own

violin up again. She is enjoying it every bit as much as she did in high school—which is more than you can say for much of the popular music that was playing at her high school prom. That's not so much because the music is different—the kind of play is different. It is almost a shame that we use the same word for both experiences. Playing the violin, after those initial years of work and frustration and very often tears, never stops being satisfying.

How should we describe this curve, so different from the pattern of purchases and addictions? I've come to call it the pattern of practices. This curve describes the satisfaction that comes from a practice: an endeavor that starts out difficult, even positively painful, but over time becomes rewarding. It can apply to learning to cook, learning to garden, learning to paint; learning to play tennis, golf, or basketball; it can apply to becoming a doctor or becoming a scuba diver.

The differences between purchases (playing an MP3) and practices (playing a violin) don't stop with the different satisfaction curves each delivers. Purchases almost always involve consuming something someone else has created. Practices almost always result in the creation of something that was not there before. Even if the only thing your practice creates is a slightly out-of-tune rendering of "Twinkle, Twinkle, Little Star," that rendition, however beautiful or flawed, only comes into existence because you take the risk of playing it. With purchases, on the other hand, all the hard work of creating has been done for you.

And this points to an even more significant difference between purchases and practices. Practices, done consistently over time, expand our own capacities in fundamental and irreversible ways. Practice the violin for an hour a day, for twenty years, and at the end you will be able to do things, to create things, you were completely unable to do and create before. Listen to recorded violin music for the same amount of time and, while you may by the end have a pretty complete mental grasp of the violin repertoire, you will be just as helpless with an actual violin as you were twenty years earlier. When we purchase, we are simply freeloading off the capacities some other person has developed, and our own capacities change very little or, most often, not at all. But when we practice, we change.

There's another intriguing difference between the pattern of purchases and the pattern of practices. Purchases, at their most exhilarating and satisfying, give us a taste of godlike control over the world. I press play on my iPod, and Yo-Yo Ma or Radiohead instantly begins playing at my command. I pull up to the drive-through window, and food is provided for me in an instantaneous exchange that requires nothing of me except my wallet and my wishes.

But practices, especially at the outset, are almost always humbling experiences of *creatureliness*. It took me months of practice before I could successfully return my coach's squash serve (and it didn't help my ego that she was a girl!). When I was learning to bake chocolate chip cookies, I forgot the baking soda half a dozen times (or substituted baking powder instead—is there a difference?). Growing tired of the simple, even monotonous exercises that are the rudiments of the piano, I'd start goofing off, drawing a rebuke from my mom, who was listening with growing impatience from the kitchen. There is nothing especially notable or admirable about someone beginning a practice— we would never pay to watch even a professional musician play scales, let alone an eight-year-old. If purchases give us an absurdly elevated sense of our command, practices cut us down to size.

And yet over time, practices lead, much more surely than purchases, to freedom. Since I, unlike my wife, have never practiced the violin, I am not free to play the violin. Put a violin in my hand and I can do nothing except hold it gingerly and try not to harm it. Meanwhile, a life built around purchases, even ones that do not lead to the deadly downward spiral of addiction, is often a life of shrinking capacity, leading to more and more constrained freedom. I become dependent on the things I buy—my iPod becomes a mood-altering device, my wardrobe becomes my identity, my car gives me a sense of power and control.

With their quick reliable hits of satisfaction, purchases are seductive. Building our life around them almost guarantees that we will never take the risk of embracing practices, which call us to long-sustained difficulties and deferred gratification. But if we build our lives around practices, if our lives are defined by choosing what is initially difficult and staying committed to it over time, not only will the practices deliver long-lasting satisfaction, our purchases will take on a new and more satisfying quality. When my wife listens to a recording of the violinist Itzhak Perlman, she enjoys it in a way that I cannot, because she quite literally hears qualities in the recording that I cannot. She can appreciate the years of discipline, concentration, and creativity that go into Perlman's seemingly effortless playing. And in our house it works the other way around as well: having spent several decades studying and performing folk, pop, jazz, and gospel on the piano, when I buy a recording that features the terrific Nashville session pianist Matt Rollings, I swoon over his inventive chord structures and breathtaking rhythmic precision, while Catherine simply taps her toes and hums along.

But a life of practices doesn't just equip us to appreciate the nuances of our particular field of expertise—violin for Catherine, piano for me, maybe tennis, vegetarian cuisine, or woodworking for you. It reorients us toward a different kind of satisfaction, freeing us from looking to purchases to shore up our sense of well-being. When you build your life around practices, purchases are satisfying without being, well, consuming. When you build your life around purchases, practices and their deeper joys always stay out of sight, and even more surely out of reach.

THE DISENCHANTED CONSUMER

Surprisingly enough, I believe there are some strong reasons to believe that our culture is becoming disenchanted with the pattern of purchases. Just as citizenship, as a defining ideal, began to wane when the post-war economy served up an abundant smorgasbord of enticing consumer goods, so I believe we can see signs that Americans' love affair with effortless consumption is growing cold. Many of our neighbors are discovering that the passivity of the consumer is unfulfilling. And just as a massive economic shift and novel technologies made the consumer economy possible, so new technologies are offering a new kind of satisfaction: the satisfaction not of consumption but of *participation*, and even *creation*.

Think about the paradigmatic change in "screen time" that has taken place in the last twenty-five

I'VE LOST COUNT OF HOW MANY PEOPLE HAVE TOLD ME THEY HAVE GROWN DISSATISFIED WITH JUST BEING CRITICS OR CONSUMERS OF CULTURE. WE ARE EAGER TO MOVE BEYOND A PASSIVE, REACTIVE POSTURE TOWARD THE CULTURE AROUND US—WE'VE REALIZED IT'S NO GOOD EITHER FOR THE CHURCH'S MISSION OR FOR OUR OWN SOULS.

years. In 1983, the year before the Macintosh computer was introduced, the only screen most people owned was a television. TV was the epitome of the passive consumer economy, perfectly designed to deliver both prefabricated entertainment and advertisements for further adventures in purchasing satisfaction.

In 2008, to be sure, most Americans still have a television screen, and it is larger and flatter than ever. But it has been joined by at least two other screens that compete for attention: the personal computer and the cell phone. And even the television spends only a fraction of its time delivering broadcast media; it is just as likely to be hooked up to an Xbox as the cable box.

The new screens offer something that the television never did: the opportunity to participate in shaping your own experience. The personal computer is the gateway to the Internet, and on the Internet I am as likely to be typing or uploading as I am to be reading or downloading. On the cell phone I am as likely to talk or text as I am to listen or read. And in the increasingly immersive and realistic world of the video game, satisfaction hinges upon my action and skill, not on the prepackaged skill of someone else. It is not an accident, I think, that the most involving video game platform yet—the Nintendo Wii, which requires not just twitching thumbs but full-body participation—has also been the best-selling console of its generation.

The most successful retail enterprises in our economy have deftly followed, and enabled, this shift from passive consumption to active participation. YouTube, which according to one study accounted for 10 percent of all Internet traffic in North America last year, is built on the premise that consumers want to become creators: "What our users want to watch is themselves," YouTube founder Chad Hurley told the Associated Press. "They don't want to watch professionally produced content. *There are so many people with cameras that have the opportunity to create their own content* and so many more people with editing tools to tell their stories, we feel this is just the tip of the iceberg" (emphasis added).

Apple CEO Steve Jobs foresaw the shift away from consumption earlier and more keenly than almost anyone. Apple built its reputation for elegance and user delight by catering to a core audience of "creative" professionals such as designers and film producers. But even "consumer" Macs ship with the "iLife suite," which includes applications like iPhoto, iMovie, and GarageBand, all designed to help you actively manage your photos, movies, and latent musical skills. To be sure, GarageBand probably goes unused by the vast majority of Apple customers, but Apple understands that our aspirations have shifted. We may still spend the majority of our lives consuming (and eagerly upgrading to the latest and greatest Apple product—has anyone ever mastered the pattern of purchases better than Jobs?), but that is not how we want to see ourselves, and Apple assures us that is not how they see us. They see us as we want to see ourselves: not as consumers, but as creators (and, of course, as fantastically groovy silhouetted dancers).

And the economic result? The largest personal computer manufacturer, Dell, made a profit of $3 billion on top-line revenues of $57 billion in 2007. Apple's top-line revenues that year were only $24 billion—less than half of Dell's—but their profit was $3.5 billion, the equal of Dell's plus a cool $500 million. There is tremendous profit to be captured by treating people as creators, not consumers.

So here is my prediction: by 2100 our great-grandchildren will identify themselves in a way that will seem as strange and foreign to us as "consumer" would have seemed to our great-grandparents. The precise word they use may not be *creators*, but it will have that word's connotations of participation and personal engagement. This doesn't mean, by the way, that they will be any less consumers than we are today, just as we are just as much citizens of our country as our great-grandparents were. It simply means that their identity, the way they order their lives, and the place they seek satisfaction will have shifted from consumption to something much more like creation.

I'm seeing something very similar among Christians. I've received a remarkable response as I've traveled speaking on the topic of my new book, *Culture Making: Recovering Our Creative Calling*. One of the themes of that book, as I shared at Q in 2007, is that in recent decades the dominant postures of evangelical Christians toward culture have been critique and consumption, not cultivation or creation. I've lost count of how many people have told me they have grown dissatisfied with just being critics or consumers of culture. We are eager to move beyond a passive, reactive posture toward the culture around us—we've realized it's no good either for the church's mission or for our own souls. Christians are not only leveling critiques at the excesses of consumerism, they are coming up with creative alternatives like the Advent Conspiracy, which redirects Christmas spending toward water projects around the world with the slogan "compassion, not consumption."

In many ways this disenchantment with consumer culture, both in mainstream culture and among many Christians, is a welcome and encouraging development. Christians of all people, whose founding story begins with a call to creativity and cultivation, and whose understanding of sin begins with an act of disobedient consumption, have every reason to welcome our culture's tentative turn away from the fleeting satisfactions of purchases.

I just wish I was sure that this trend is good news.

UNDISCIPLINED CREATIVITY

For here is the problem with our turn toward participation and a kind of creative involvement: it can easily replicate the pattern of purchases

general public. (LiveJournal may seem passé today, just as Facebook probably will by this time next year, but according to Alexa, LiveJournal's worldwide traffic rank in June 2008 was still a very respectable 54.) In 2005 LiveJournal released some fascinating information about the

I JUST WISH I WAS SURE THAT THIS TREND IS GOOD NEWS.

all over again, except this time the "purchased" good is our own creativity.

Consider one of the most prodigious examples of mass creativity since the rise of the Internet: the phenomenon of weblogs, those outposts of personal expression that captured so much attention and occupied so much of the time of pajama-clad netizens in the early years of the twenty-first century. One of the early pioneers in bringing blogs to the masses, especially the teenage masses, was the website LiveJournal, which made it easy for anyone to easily broadcast their latest musings to their friends and the

blogs it hosted. Two hundred ninety thousand LiveJournal users had updated their blogs in the past thirty days (and as all bloggers know, if you haven't updated your blog in thirty days, you don't have a blog). That was 20 percent of LiveJournal's total registered users—meaning that 1.16 million LiveJournal users had effectively abandoned their blogs.

What did the satisfaction curve look like for those 1,116,000 people? Perhaps you are one of them. Do you recall the euphoria when your blog site first went live? The excitement of posting your thoughts about politics, the church, contemporary culture, the meaning of life—not to mention the most fascinating topic of all, blogging itself?

The second and third days were not quite as exciting, but of course you still had lots of pent-up creativity to express. Witty posts about your English class, updates on your plans for the weekend, a carefully crafted examination of the pros and cons of getting a new cell phone. Day four featured a photograph of your dog. Then there was the first week's traffic report, where you discovered that all your creative output had been viewed by a grand total of twenty-three people, four of whom were your mom.

The satisfaction curve of blogging, for the vast majority of bloggers, in fact looks exactly like the pattern of purchases—because for the 1.16 million LiveJournal users who abandoned their blogs, and for the tens or hundreds of millions of others whose blogs now languish in the dark entropic corners of the Internet, all blogging was ever about was self-expression.

And it turns out that self-expression, strangely enough, is not ultimately satisfying—because the selves we have to express, in an era of purchases, turn out to be depressingly shallow. Even the personally engaged, creative act of blogging, *if engaged in without discipline*, is as banal and boring as a pop song that's been on the charts for a few weeks too long.

There is a real possibility—given human nature, *probability*—that all the current enthusiasm for participation and creativity, described so accurately by Chad Hurley, will lead to just the same kind of aimless anomie as consumer culture. But this time it will carry with it a core of narcissism that will make the consumer culture seem vibrant by comparison: "What our users want to watch is themselves." We will watch ourselves, and because we have done nothing to cultivate or shape our selves, what we watch will be as initially titillating and ultimately empty as any consumer purchase ever was.

Without practices, even creativity is in the long run unsatisfying. Millions of former bloggers will tell you so.

CHOOSING OUR WAY

So here is the opportunity of our moment: to capture our neighbors' dissatisfaction with the consumer culture, and our own, and take up a long-standing invitation to a more excellent way.

In the pattern of practices, we find an inescapable parallel to one of the essential elements of the ministry of Jesus. Another word for *practice*, of course, is *discipline*, and those who embrace disciplines are disciples. The pattern of practices is perfectly and profoundly summarized by Jesus for his disciples in Mark 8:34–35: "Whoever wants to be my disciple must deny themselves and take up their cross and follow me.

For whoever wants to save their life will lose it, but whoever loses their life for me and for the gospel will save it." In Mark's story, Jesus has just performed two remarkable miracles that have everything to do with consumption: he has taken a few loaves and fish and fed crowds of five thousand, then four thousand. Hunger has been instantly and miraculously satisfied—a kind of divine drive-through window—but Jesus immediately serves notice that his way is not the way of consumption but discipline. The feasts for thousands are not a pattern—there will not be a daily free meal served up with no expectations and no questions asked—but a gift and a sign. The meals and their leftovers are a down payment on a future abundant life, a glimpse of the joy that is coming, but the way to that life is going to be sacrifice, not self-fulfillment.

What is behind the pattern of purchases, after all, but the belief that the best way to save our lives is to grab all the satisfaction we can, as quickly as we can? And what is the pattern of practices but the willingness to lose our lives, to abandon short-term satisfaction, trusting that eventually our lives will be saved and we will be more deeply satisfied than we can imagine? As the writer to the Hebrews puts it, Jesus, "for the joy set before him he endured the cross, scorning its shame, and"—only then—"sat down at the right hand of the throne of God" (Heb. 12:2).

So what is at stake, ultimately, in our culture's embrace of the pattern of purchases is our ability to recognize the invitation of Jesus as good news. To people whose lives are built on the purchase model of satisfaction, the invitation to practices seems like—and is—an invitation to lose our lives. We recoil at the thought that Jesus might not be all that interested in our self-expression, but might rather be inviting us into a costly life of practice that could ultimately form us into the kind of people who would have a self worth expressing. And Jesus' costly life might prove to be the only real path to satisfaction, the only way to keep our heads and hearts sane in the midst of a riot of consumable goods—able, like Jesus himself, both to feast and to fast joyfully, without becoming captive either to excess or asceticism.

If there is one worry I have about the enthusiastic response so far to *Culture Making*, it is that too many of its readers (and very possibly its writer) will race off to become culture makers—hurrying along to embrace the call to creativity without counting the cost. Along the way, we will cheapen the true glory of creativity in much the same way that the grave and glad duty of *citizens* has somehow been reduced to the mass mechanical role of *voters*. We will join our neighbors in orgies of self-expression, gamely trying to bring a Christian creative presence into our culture, without allowing Christ to be formed in us, allowing our selves to be taken up into his incomparable life. We will skip over the hard work of practices—whether the spiritual disciplines of fasting, solitude, and silence, or the cultural disciplines specific to every vocation that require years or decades of preparation and training.

But perhaps some of us are ready to hear Jesus' call. We are weary of the constant drumbeat of consumption or the constant effort to gin up our own creativity. Perhaps we have tasted the bitter fruit of addiction, so sweet at the start and so soon stale, and are ready for something more real and lasting. Perhaps we were lucky enough to be schooled in a practice early in our lives—the hours of practice on an instrument; the wind sprints on the field behind the school at 7 a.m.; the rehearsals over and over of a line, a piece of dialogue, a scene—and can still recall how good it was to live that way, how much better that was than our consumptive distracted lives have become. Perhaps we have glimpsed Jesus incomparably alive in the most unlikely places, the places we would never go among the people we would consider the most unsatisfying. If we are willing to follow him there, we could still become the citizens, the creators—and even the consumers—we were meant to be.

Andy Crouch is the author of Culture Making: Recovering Our Creative Calling, *winner of* Christianity Today's *2009 Book Award for Christianity and Culture. He is also a senior editor at* Christianity Today International, *a member of the editorial board of* Books & Culture, *and a senior fellow of the International Justice Mission's IJM Institute.*

JOURNAL

In a consumer society there are inevitably two kinds of slaves: the prisoners of addiction and the prisoners of envy.

IVAN ILLICH

You do anything long enough to escape the habit of living until the escape becomes the habit.

DAVID RYAN

The two most powerful warriors are patience and time.

LEO TOLSTOY

GROUP GATHERING TWO

FROM PURCHASES TO PRACTICES

YOU ARE A CONSUMER

DISCUSS

Believe it or not, there was a time when American society was largely characterized by civic participation. But Andy Crouch asserts that we now live in consumer-based culture: "On a daily basis, the place where we find meaning and satisfaction is not primarily in civic participation, but in consumption."

DISCUSSION STARTERS

In what ways are most of the choices in your life guided by consumption?

How does the dominance of advertising in our culture influence your decisions and behaviors?

How has a consumeristic mentality shaped our posture toward the church, faith, and spirituality?

WHERE THE AVERAGE AMERICAN FAMILY SPENDS ITS INCOME

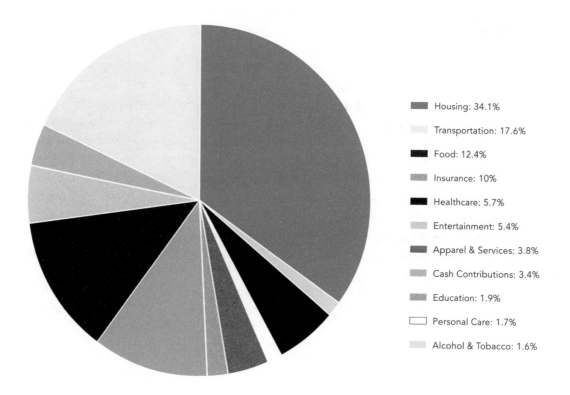

- Housing: 34.1%
- Transportation: 17.6%
- Food: 12.4%
- Insurance: 10%
- Healthcare: 5.7%
- Entertainment: 5.4%
- Apparel & Services: 3.8%
- Cash Contributions: 3.4%
- Education: 1.9%
- Personal Care: 1.7%
- Alcohol & Tobacco: 1.6%

Source: U.S. Dept. of Labor, U.S. Bureau of Labor Statistics: "Consumer Expenditures," April, 2009 at http://www.visualeconomics.com/how-the-average-us-consumer-spends-their-paycheck/.

HOW DOES THE CHURCH RESPOND?

DEBATE

Split the group into two sides and spend fifteen minutes debating the issue:

Should the church adapt the presentation of its message to reach consumers in our culture, or must churches forsake any methods that cater to a consumer mentality?

Record your thoughts on each position on pages 50-51.

Use the following debate starters to guide your time.

Few would disagree that American culture is consumeristic. But what about the American church? In an age when people demand the best products and experiences for the money and time they spend, have American churches adopted this mentality by turning the gospel message into a product and the weekend worship service into a production experience? Perhaps this is necessary for the sake of contextualization. Or perhaps this represents the very problem that Andy Crouch highlights and explains why many are finding new expressions of church unsatisfying. Which is it?

Should the church adapt the presentation of its message to reach consumers in our culture, or must churches forsake any methods that cater to a consumer mentality?

DEBATE STARTERS

Paul wrote: "Though I am free and belong to no one, I have made myself a slave to everyone, to win as many as possible. To the Jews I became like a Jew, to win the Jews. To those under the law I became like one under the law.... To those not having the law I became like one not having the law.... To the weak I became weak.... I have become all things to all people so that by all possible means I might save some" (1 Cor. 9:19–22). Doesn't this suggest that we should do whatever it takes—even yielding to consumer culture—to introduce people to the gospel message?

Which is more important: what the church is attracting people with, or what the church is attracting people to? Is there a connection between the two?

Some suggest that the pattern of Jesus' ministry was to meet people where they were. Others propose that Jesus unashamedly challenged followers to count the cost and forsake their selfish desires. Which is right? Is it possible to maintain a balance?

Practically speaking, should attending a church service resemble more of a purchase or a practice? What are the implications of seeing it through either of these lenses?

—

YES

The American church should adapt the presentation of its message to reach consumers in our culture.

THOUGHTS

—

NO

American churches should forsake any methods that cater to a consumer mentality.

THOUGHTS

—

WE ARE NOT TOURISTS

—

Have a few people in your group take turns reading this section aloud.

Consumer culture is built upon making purchases. But Andy Crouch warns, "With their quick reliable hits of satisfaction, purchases are seductive. Building our life around them almost guarantees that we will never take the risk of embracing practices, which call us to long-sustained difficulties and deferred gratification."

Pastor and writer Eugene Peterson echoes the same sentiments and explains the underlying problem:

> One aspect of [our] world that I have been able to identify as harmful to Christians is the assumption that anything worthwhile can be acquired at once. We assume that if something can be done at all, it can be done quickly and efficiently. Our attention spans have been conditioned by thirty-second commercials. Our sense of reality has been flattened by thirty-page abridgments.
>
> It is not difficult in such a world to get a person interested in the message of the gospel; it is terribly difficult to sustain the interest. Millions of people in our culture make decisions for Christ, but there is a dreadful attrition rate. Many claim to have been born again, but the evidence for mature Christian

discipleship is slim. In our kind of culture anything, even news about God, can be sold if it is packaged freshly; but when it loses its novelty, it goes on the garbage heap. There is a great market for religious experience in our world; there is little enthusiasm for the patient acquisition of virtue, little inclination to sign up for a long apprenticeship in what earlier generations of Christians called holiness.

Religion in our time has been captured by the tourist mindset. Religion is understood as a visit to an attractive site to be made when we have adequate leisure. For some it is a weekly jaunt to church. For others, occasional visits to special services. Some, with a bent for religious entertainment and sacred diversion, plan their lives around special events like retreats, rallies and conferences. We go to see a new personality, to hear a new truth, to get a new experience and so, somehow, expand our otherwise humdrum lives.... We'll try anything—until something else comes along.

I don't know what it has been like for pastors in other cultures and previous centuries, but ... the persons whom I lead in worship, among whom I counsel, visit, pray, preach, and teach, want shortcuts. They want me to help them fill out the form that will get them instant credit (in eternity). They are impatient for results. They have adopted the lifestyle of a tourist and only want the high points. But a pastor is not a tour guide.... The Christian life cannot mature under such conditions and in such ways.

Friedrich Nietzsche, who saw this area of spiritual truth, at least, with great clarity wrote, "The essential thing 'in heaven and earth' is ... that there should be a long obedience in the same direction; there thereby results, and has always resulted in the long run, something which has made life worth living" (*Beyond Good and Evil*, trans. Helen Zimmern [London, 1907], Section 188, pp. 106–9). It is this "long obedience in the same direction" which the mood of the world does so much to discourage. (*A Long Obedience in the Same Direction*, InterVarsity Press, 1980, pp. 11–13)

REFLECTION STARTERS

Spend a few minutes journaling your thoughts to the two questions below. Then, share your reflections with the group.

In what ways are you tempted to organize your spiritual life around a "pattern of purchases" or "shortcuts to instant results"?

What practices do you believe would make you a more creative and faithful follower of Christ over time? What kind of support would you need to embrace those practices? What would you have to give up to begin practicing them?

JOURNAL

A LONG OBEDIENCE

ACT

Growing into the people that God made and called us to be is a process. It is slow and sometimes difficult. It is a process that is facilitated by the regular practice of disciplines that form and transform over time. And it requires of us "a long obedience in the same direction." But the result is genuine satisfaction, contentment, freedom, and peace. Not because we've accomplished something. But because we've truly communed with our Creator and Savior in the process. A long and fulfilling journey is just as important as the destination.

How could your church become a place that persuades people that true long-term satisfaction is found in the obedience of practices, not the short-term gratification of purchases?

THE SPIRITUALITY OF THE CELL PHONE

There are many barriers that prevent us from embracing transformative practices in our lives. We are busy, distracted people. And nothing adds to our busyness and distractions more than technology. Every day, we are bombarded with emails, phone calls, text messages, Facebook and Twitter updates—all competing for our time and attention. Between now and your next gathering, spend fifteen minutes every morning with God. Before you check email, surf the Internet, turn on the television, or work on your to-do list, find a quiet place to read a passage of Scripture, meditate, and pray. Use Psalm 23 as a guide.

Spend the final portion of your time together discussing your culture-shaping project.

PREPARING FOR YOUR CULTURE-SHAPING PROJECT

In the next few weeks, your group will take part in a project together to apply what you are learning and discussing. It's important that you complete this project before your last gathering. Three options for what your group can do have been recommended on pages 94-95. All of them require some planning and preparation. Take a few minutes now to read the options and discuss which one best suits your group. You don't have to make a decision this week, but you need to get the ball rolling and be prepared to make a decision and start planning at your next group meeting.

Today convenience is the success factor of just about every type of product and service that is showing steady growth.

CHARLES MORTIMER

One of the many reasons for the bewildering and tragic character of human existence is the fact that social organization is at once necessary and fatal. Men are forever creating such organizations for their own convenience and forever finding themselves the victims of their home-made monsters.

ALDOUS HUXLEY

What good is it for someone to gain the whole world, yet forfeit their soul?

MARK 8:36

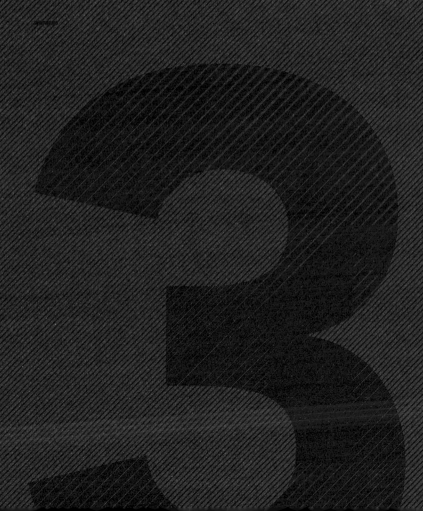

GROUP GATHERING THREE

THE SPIRITUALITY OF THE CELL PHONE

YOUR TECHNOLOGY

DISCUSS

Spend a few minutes sharing your thoughts with the group.

It's been said that technology now governs so much of our lives—for good or for bad. In what ways do technological devices govern your life?

DISCUSSION STARTERS

What kind of mobile phone or personal digital device do you own? How often do you use it each day and for what purposes?

Do you use Facebook, Twitter, or some other social networking medium? What are the benefits you've experienced from them? What are the drawbacks?

Estimate how much time you typically spend each day watching television, using the Internet, or communicating with others via long-distance media like the phone, email, text messages, or social networking. Do you think it's too much? Why or why not?

MONTHLY USE OF MOBILE PHONES BY AVERAGE AMERICANS

Monthly Voice and Text Usage By Age

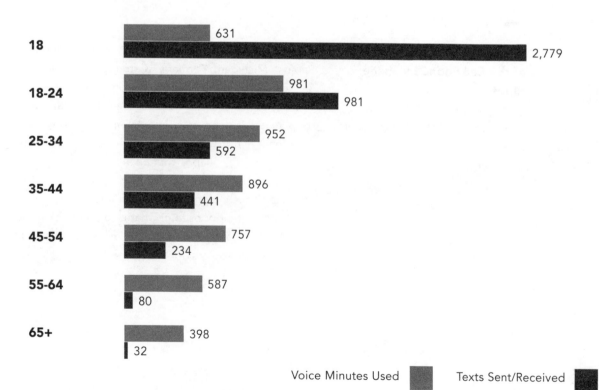

Age		
18	631	2,779
18-24	981	981
25-34	952	592
35-44	896	441
45-54	757	234
55-64	587	80
65+	398	32

Voice Minutes Used   Texts Sent/Received

Source: The Neilsen Company, April 2009–March 2010

THE SPIRITUALITY OF THE CELL PHONE

WATCH

View Q Talk: The Spirituality of the Cell Phone by Shane Hipps.

Record your thoughts on the talk on page 65.

Shane Hipps is a teaching pastor at Mars Hill Bible Church in Grand Rapids, Michigan. Formerly a strategic planner in advertising, Shane spent several years working on the communications strategy for Porsche Cars North America. He later left advertising to pursue his long-held interest in spirituality, theology, and vocational ministry. Shane is also the author of *Flickering Pixels: How Technology Shapes Your Faith*.

Our use of technology creates a relationship to time and space that is often the opposite of what is required for spiritual growth. At Q Austin, Shane explored the unintended effects of technology on our souls in today's digital age.

—

"Every single thing about this technological age is simply the culmination of all human ingenuity and all human creativity throughout all of time."

—

"Our technological diet shapes the soul as much as the food diet shapes the body."

—

"What the cell phone does is it creates a relationship to time that is exactly the opposite of the one required for spiritual growth and development and wholeness."

—

"In a world of absence, we are called to be presence. We are called to incarnate Christ in a discarnate age."

—

"Our capacity to experience God and our capacity to have impact in the world is directly related to our relationship to time and space."

THOUGHTS

MORE EFFICIENT OR MORE DEFICIENT?

Split the group into two sides and spend fifteen minutes debating the issue:

Does our dependence on technologies like the cell phone make us more efficient, and therefore better, humans? Or more deficient for whom God has called us to be?

Even if you don't agree with the side you are representing, consider and offer the best arguments for your position. Be respectful.

Record your thoughts on pages 68-69.

Use the following debate starters to guide your time.

Shane Hipps asserts that the way we use our cell phones (and other forms of technology) creates an unhealthy relationship to both time and space. In our desire to be more efficient, we embrace a more disembodied existence that prevents us from fully experiencing God and being fully present to others. Is he right or is he just being a Luddite?

Does our dependence on technologies like the cell phone make us more efficient, and therefore better, humans? Or more deficient for whom God has called us to be?

DEBATE STARTERS

Don't cell phones give us more or better ability to communicate with friends, family, and others who we might not otherwise connect with regularly?

Does the quality of our relationships suffer when we primarily use email, text messages, and status updates to communicate with others?

How do the ways that we know, connect with, and relate to others influence the ways we know, connect with, and relate to God?

Does Shane's argument suggest that we should entirely avoid all new forms of technology that may negatively impact who God made us to be? Or is there a balance to be found? If so, how?

—

YES

Technologies like the cell phone make us more efficient, and therefore better, humans.

THOUGHTS

—

NO

Technologies like the cell phone make us more distracted and deficient for whom God has called us to be.

THOUGHTS

CHOOSING EMBODIMENT

Have a few people in the group take turns reading this section aloud.

During your first group gathering, Phyllis Tickle introduced the importance of ancient disciplines in our spiritual formation. Then, Andy Crouch suggested that pursuing these disciplines (or practices) stands in stark contrast to the immediate gratification of purchases we make in our consumer-oriented culture. But the practices, he asserts, are more essential and fulfilling, even if more demanding, for following Christ with our whole beings and lives.

The question of how technology shapes us may seem like a hard right turn, but the connection is vital. If our use of cell phones (or computers, cars, microwave ovens, etc.) has a profound effect for governing the ways we think and act, then we must evaluate when technology creates a more healthy formation of our relationship to God and to others, and when it doesn't.

One of the concerns is that communicating with others via phone, emails, text messages, or status updates promotes disembodiment. We aren't fully present with others when we rely so heavily on these forms of communication. In *The Next Christians* (pp. 141-143), Gabe Lyons shares about lessons he learned regarding this danger from his friend Kevin Kelly:

Visiting Kevin Kelly, a heralded futurist and senior writer for *Wired* magazine, at his home taught me a lot about embodiment. Kevin's work sits at the heart of technology innovation. If you didn't know him, you might assume he lives in a digital paradise—constantly online, voraciously keeping up with the latest new trends, a real mad scientist of sorts. But Kevin's life exhibits the complete opposite.

As we talked in his home office loft, the signs all around of his eccentricity and the nonconformist way he chooses to live refreshed me. He doesn't use a cell phone, has never twittered, rides his bike for transportation, and doesn't even own a laptop. Sure, he still has the attributes of a crazed inventor; we sat together underneath his hanging space models, alongside ant farms and amid mounds of clutter that evolves when an innovator does his best work. (Not to mention, I was greeted at his door by a ten-foot-tall Styrofoam robot, just as unusual as its inventor.) But Kevin's simple life represents a complete anomaly; it's not how most of us would expect a futurist like him to live, and that's the point ...

While choosing embodiment may seem like one of the toughest disciplines to practice, Kevin has devised a few basic rules to help make it work. They seem to be useful for any Christian serious about this practice. He explains how he applies embodiment amid the onslaught of email, phone calls, and demands of modern life:

My first priority is face-to-face conversation. If I can be physically in front of someone, I give that person my full attention—ignoring competing distractions of phone calls or anything else that might hinder my focus. But if a face-to-face conversation is not possible, I defer to voice-to-voice—normally by way of the phone. But even with that, I have rules. When I'm having a phone conversation, I don't look at my computer screen or engage with anything in front of me, except the person I'm talking to at that very moment. I want to be fully present. But finally, if neither one of those options exist, my last resort is screen-to-screen. Using email or sending a text is my last preference—but even then I keep it short and sweet but force myself to be fully present in the written communication I send.

REFLECTION STARTERS

Spend a few minutes journaling your thoughts to the two questions below. Then, share your reflections with the group.

How do Kevin Kelly's suggestions about prioritizing embodiment when relating to others challenge you?

What would you have to give up in order to embrace a practice like this? Is it worth it?

JOURNAL

—

BEING THOUGHTFUL

ACT

—

Technology isn't inherently evil. But it does have its negative biases. And unless we are aware of those dangers, we'll be ignorant of the barriers that may keep us from relating to God and others in the ways we were created to do so.

What one discipline related to technology do you intend to begin practicing and how can your group support you in that endeavor?

OBSERVING THE SABBATH

One important practice in particular is extremely easy to neglect in our productivity-obsessed culture: keeping the Sabbath. Before your next group gathering, set aside one day (it doesn't have to be Sunday) to "keep the Sabbath." During this twenty-four-hour period, take a complete break from anything that is considered work for you. Spend time with family, friends, or alone with God, but don't do anything "productive."

Spend the final portion of your time together discussing your culture-shaping project.

PLANNING THE CULTURE-SHAPING PROJECT

You'll need to make a decision by the end of this gathering since what you do will likely require planning. Your project needs to take place before your last group gathering and it should be something that everyone can participate in. You can review the suggestions given on pages 94-95. It may be difficult to find total agreement among the group, but try to establish some consensus by talking through the advantages and disadvantages of all suggestions. Don't be afraid to think creatively and challenge yourselves. You're not limited by the suggestions included in this study, but you'll want to undertake something that will help you apply what you've been learning. Make a decision and solidify action steps before you conclude.

Lord, you have made us for yourself, and our hearts are restless until they rest in you.

AUGUSTINE

The best of all medicines is resting and fasting.

BENJAMIN FRANKLIN

Do not let Sunday be taken from you. If your soul has no Sunday, it becomes an orphan.

ALBERT SCHWEITZER

OBSERVING THE SABBATH

—

YOUR SABBATH

—

Spend a few minutes sharing your thoughts with the group.

What is your past experience with the concept of keeping the Sabbath? And did you follow the assignment and take a day of Sabbath rest before this group gathering? If so, what did you experience?

DISCUSSION STARTERS

Keeping the Sabbath has often been associated with attending church on Sunday. Has this been your understanding? Why or why not?

Has keeping the Sabbath been a practice for you in the past? If so, what have you done to make this possible? If not, why not?

How difficult was it for you to schedule a day of Sabbath rest before this group gathering and carry it through?

THE TEN COMMANDMENTS (EXODUS 20:3–17)

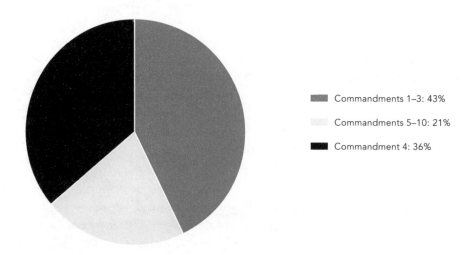

Commandments 1–3: 43%

Commandments 5–10: 21%

Commandment 4: 36%

COMMANDMENT FOUR:

"Remember the Sabbath day by keeping it holy. Six days you shall labor and do all your work, but the seventh day is a sabbath to the LORD your God. On it you shall not do any work, neither you, nor your son or daughter, nor your male or female servant, nor your animals, nor any foreigner residing in your towns. For in six days the LORD made the heavens and the earth, the sea, and all that is in them, but he rested on the seventh day. Therefore the LORD blessed the Sabbath day and made it holy."

OBERVING THE SABBATH

WATCH

View Q Talk: Observing the Sabbath by Matthew Sleeth.

Record your thoughts on the talk on page 83.

Dr. Matthew Sleeth resigned from his hospital position as chief of the medical staff and director of the ER to lecture, write, and preach about creation care and the environment. Dr. Sleeth is the author of *Serve God, Save the Planet: A Christian Call to Action* and *The Gospel According to the Earth: Why the Good Book Is a Green Book.*

Are Christians really supposed to keep the Sabbath, or is that just an Old Testament idea with no meaning in our world today? If we did, what would be the effect on our families, our health, our consumption, and our world? At Q Chicago, Matthew Sleeth imagined what role the Sabbath might play in a restored life in the twenty-first century.

—

"In a 24/7 world, rest is not going to happen unless you plan for it."

—

"How many of you take one day a week, put it in park, and give it to the LORD?"

—

"Christ says, 'We're not meant to save Sabbath, Sabbath is meant to save us.' "

—

"Rest: figure out what work is for you, and don't do it."

THOUGHTS

CAN WE TAKE THIS TOO FAR?

DEBATE

Split the group into two sides and spend fifteen minutes debating the issue:

Can we take this idea of keeping the Sabbath too far and turn it into an unrealistic and legalistic rule?

Even if you don't agree with the side you are representing, consider and offer the best arguments for your position. Be respectful.

Record your thoughts on pages 86-87.

Use the following debate starters to guide your time.

Few people argue with the idea of the Sabbath. It's important to experience regular rest in our lives. There's plenty of medical evidence to support the fact that our minds and bodies need it. So there's not really a question of whether or not keeping the Sabbath is a good idea. The question is how. Is it possible to take this definition of "figure out what work is for you, and don't do it" too far? What if "work" for you is taking care of your children, mowing the yard, cleaning the house, or preparing meals? Do you avoid all of these things as well? Is it possible to become legalistic about this?

Can we take this idea of keeping the Sabbath too far and turn it into an unrealistic and legalistic rule?

DEBATE STARTERS

The command to keep the Sabbath isn't explicitly reaffirmed in the New Testament while many of the other Ten Commandments are. Does this mean that Christians are no longer bound to keep this practice?

How would you define "work" in your life? Is it possible or realistic to entirely cease from it one day a week?

What are the potential negative consequences of completely ceasing from "work" one day a week?

What are the potential long-term benefits of making a commitment to regularly keeping a Sabbath?

—

YES

It's just not realistic to cease from anything we consider work one day a week, nor is it healthy.

THOUGHTS

—

NO

The commandment to keep the Sabbath may seem extreme, but the long-term benefits are worth the sacrifice.

THOUGHTS

—

EXPANDING THE SABBATH

—

Have a few people in the group take turns reading this section aloud.

So far, we've discussed Sabbath in terms of resting one day a week. But there are two other related concepts found in the Bible. First, the Israelites were also instructed to keep a Sabbath year once every seven years:

> The LORD said to Moses on Mount Sinai, "Speak to the Israelites and say to them: 'When you enter the land I am going to give you, the land itself must observe a sabbath to the LORD. For six years sow your fields, and for six years prune your vineyards and gather their crops. But in the seventh year the land is to have a year of sabbath rest, a sabbath to the LORD. Do not sow your fields or prune your vineyards. Do not reap what grows of itself or harvest the grapes of your untended vines. The land is to have a year of rest. Whatever the land yields during the sabbath year will be food for you—for yourself, your male and female servants, and the hired worker and temporary resident who live among you, as well as for your livestock and the wild animals in your land. Whatever the land produces may be eaten."
>
> –Leviticus 25:1–7

Second, the writer of the book of Hebrews refers to a general Sabbath-rest that all followers of Christ should experience:

> Therefore, since the promise of entering his rest still stands, let us be careful that none of you be found to have fallen short of it. For we also have had the good news proclaimed to us, just as [the disobedient Israelites who wandered in the wilderness] did; but the message they heard was of no value to them, because they did not share the faith of those who obeyed....
>
> There remains, then, a Sabbath-rest for the people of God; for anyone who enter God's rest also rests from their works, just as God did from his. Let us, therefore, make every effort to enter that rest, so that no one will perish by following their example of disobedience.

–Hebrews 4:1–2, 9–11

REFLECTION STARTERS

Spend a few minutes journaling your thoughts to the two questions below. Then, share your reflections with the group.

Is it important for you to take extended times of rest (a week, a month, a season) in your life when you cease from your work and trust that God will provide? If so, do you do this? If not, why not?

If becoming a follower of Christ should produce an overall and enduring sense of inner peace and rest, what are the things in our lives that endanger this orientation?

JOURNAL

JOURNAL

AN ESSENTIAL PRACTICE

ACT

Keeping the Sabbath isn't just a commandment we should follow out of obedience. It renews our dependence on God. It forces us to stop and realize that there is more to our lives than what we do or produce. The Sabbath paves the way for experiencing meaningful relationships with others and with God himself. It's not easy, and it requires sacrifice. But keeping the Sabbath is an essential practice that regularly shapes us into the people God created us to be.

What practical steps will you take to make keeping the Sabbath a priority in your life?

—

CULTURE-SHAPING PROJECT

PREPARE FOR NEXT GATHERING

—

Your primary assignment is to undertake your culture-shaping project before your next gathering. Be intentional about setting aside time to prepare for and execute your project so that you can discuss it when you next meet. Project options follow on pages 94-95.

CULTURE-SHAPING PROJECT

IDEAS FOR GROUP PROJECT

Your group has been discussing rediscovering ancient practices of the faith. Now you have an opportunity to take what you are learning and do something together. Be sure to plan this group project early and undertake it before your final group gathering. Following are three options you might consider.

Option One: Practice Fixed-Hour Prayer Together

Phyllis Tickle mentioned the practice of fixed-hour prayer. This includes praying at three times throughout the day: morning prayers, midday prayers, and evening prayers. As a group, for one week, commit to this practice. Also, invite a friend outside of your group or at work to do this project with you. It will feel odd and foreign for some, but commit to giving it a try. You won't be physically together, but you'll know that each person in the group (along with countless others) will be quietly praying together at the same time. Go to *www.explorefaith.org/prayer/fixed/* and "Pray the Hours" for guidance on the specific prayers to use at each time.

Option Two: Communication Technology "Fast"

As a group, abstain from using the technology of email, text messaging, and social media (e.g., Facebook and Twitter) for an entire week (except for essential work-related communication). In other words, only communicate socially with others in person or over the phone. You *can* do it. It may seem like an inconvenience, and it is. But make the appropriate preparations ahead of time and just do it. Explain to others—in your "vacation reply" email—that you are taking part in an experiment and would be happy to talk with them on the phone or in person. Focus on being fully present in relationships and come prepared to discuss what you learned from your technology "fast" at the next gathering.

Option Three: Meeting with an Orthodox Rabbi

It's no surprise that many of the ancient practices of the Christian faith find their origins in Judaism. And today, Orthodox Jews still make ancient disciplines a foundation of their faith. Contact a local Orthodox Jewish rabbi and schedule a time to meet with him as a group. Ask him about his understanding of the Sabbath and other practices or rituals that embody the Jewish faith. Set aside theological differences and seek to learn how those of a different, though related, faith meaningfully incorporate disciplines into their lives.

A humble understanding of yourself is a surer way to God than a profound searching after knowledge.

THOMAS À KEMPIS

No evil propensity of the human heart is so powerful that it may not be subdued by discipline.

SENECA

Stand firm, and you will win life.

LUKE 21:19

EVALUATING THE PROJECT

DISCUSS

Over the past several weeks, you've been exposed to some new ideas. Your group has discussed and debated how these concepts might change the way you think about faith and culture. And you've worked on a group project together to begin considering how these ideas might change the way you live your lives. Spend some time evaluating what you learned during your group project.

DISCUSSION STARTERS

How difficult was it to undertake your group project?

Did you find any part of it uncomfortable or not helpful? Why?

What's the most important thing you learned during your group project?

What are the biggest barriers for you personally to stay disciplined in incorporating some of these ancient practices in your life?

THOUGHTS

BUILDING YOUR HOUSE ON THE ROCK

REFLECT

Have a few people in the group take turns reading this section aloud.

In Jesus' famous Sermon on the Mount (Matthew 5–7), he taught his disciples what it meant to truly follow him and live a kingdom-oriented life. Much of his teaching must have seemed radical and overwhelming to them. "Blessed are those who mourn." "Love your enemies." "Be perfect, therefore, as your heavenly Father is perfect." "You cannot serve both God and Money." "Do not worry about your life." "Do not judge." The disciples surely concluded: *How can anyone really do all these things?*

You may have the same thought as you come to the end of this study. *Is it really realistic to begin trying to incorporate all these practices into my life?* No, it's not. But neither is it about *trying*, to begin with. As John Ortberg so helpfully writes: "There is an immense difference between *training* to do something and *trying* to do something.... For much of my life, when I heard messages about following Jesus, I thought in terms of *trying hard* to be like him.... [But] spiritual transformation is not a matter of trying harder, but training wisely" (*The Life You've Always Wanted*, Zondervan, 2002, p. 43).

Perhaps that's why Jesus concluded the Sermon on the Mount with this story:

> Therefore everyone who hears these words of mine and puts them into practice is like a wise man who built his house on the rock. The rain came down, the streams rose, and the winds blew and beat against that house; yet it did not fall, because it had its foundation on the rock. But everyone who hears these words of mine and does not put them into practice is like a foolish man who built his house on sand. The rain came down, the streams rose, and the winds blew and beat against that house, and it fell with a great crash.
>
> –Matthew 7:24–27

Beginning to put some of these disciplines into practice in your life is not about trying to be like Jesus or getting on God's good side by doing things that earn his favor. Rather, the central purpose of the ancient practices is that they *ground* us. They keep us anchored to God in a culture that pulls us in so many other directions. They shape our priorities, prepare us for hardship, and keep us rooted in God's grace. Without them, we become untethered. With them, we face the storms of life, the pressures of work, and the unsatisfying currents of culture with a sure foundation. Not because of anything we've done, but because we remain firmly in the hands of our strong Creator and Redeemer.

REFLECTION STARTERS

Spend a few minutes journaling your thoughts to these questions, then share with the group.

How does this distinction between training and trying help you process the place of practices in your life?

In what areas of your life do you feel like you need more grounding?

JOURNAL

GO AND PRACTICE

ACT

Share your final thoughts with the group about your experience during this study.

How do you view spiritual practices or disciplines differently as a result of this Q Study?

What have you learned?

What will you change about your lifestyle in the future?

What will you start doing?

What will you stop doing?

Spend the last fifteen minutes of your gathering praying as a group.

If you've never prayed out loud with other people, don't let this intimidate you. Your prayers need not be elaborate or articulate. Simply talk to God. Use these suggestions to guide your time:

- Thank God for the specific ways he has revealed himself to you during the disciplines you practiced during this study.

• Ask God to give you courage and discipline for incorporating one or more practices into your life more regularly.

• Thank God for the power he grants us to pursue these disciplines and the grace he gives when we inevitably fall short.

• Ask God for the desire, wisdom, and ability to help others in your group as they seek to embrace new practices that will ground their hearts, souls, and minds in him.

Practice. Practice. Practice.

Share Your Thoughts

With the Author: Your comments will be forwarded to
the author when you send them to *zauthor@zondervan.com*.

With Zondervan: Submit your review of this book
by writing to *zreview@zondervan.com*.

Free Online Resources at

www.zondervan.com

Zondervan AuthorTracker: Be notified whenever your favorite
authors publish new books, go on tour, or post an update
about what's happening in their lives at www.zondervan.com/
authortracker.

Daily Bible Verses and Devotions: Enrich your life with daily
Bible verses or devotions that help you start every morning
focused on God. Visit www.zondervan.com/newsletters.

Free Email Publications: Sign up for newsletters on Christian
living, academic resources, church ministry, fiction, children's
resources, and more. Visit www.zondervan.com/newsletters.

Zondervan Bible Search: Find and compare Bible passages in
a variety of translations at www.zondervanbiblesearch.com.

Other Benefits: Register yourself to receive online benefits
like coupons and special offers, or to participate in research.